I'm Lost Without You

Linda Emig

Illustrated By: Lyle Jakosalem

Print information available on the last page

Rev. date: 07/28/2015

To order additional copies of this book, contact:
Xlibris
1-888-795-4274
www.Xlibris.com
Orders@Xlibris.com

To my wonderful husband who always inspired me.

Hi, my name is Dudley. I was lost for awhile. No, not from my home; but still lost!
You see, my best friend, my favorite person to spend time with, is gone.

My adopted Daddy was very sick. He was in the hospital for a long time before I came to live with him.
When we met, I had a special feeling for him, because I could see that he was not well. I was sick too. Not the same as him. To look at me I looked o.k., but it was inside of me where I was hurt.
I came from a home where I was punished for things my owner was feeling. The man would be mean to me because he was unhappy or angry....

I would be hit, yelled at, and put outside without food or water.

The rest of the family didn't really pay any attention to me. Usually, I was just ignored. It was better than being hit or kicked, but I still longed for someone to love me.

One time, I was put outside where they tied me up and left me there. I saw them leave in a car. I wondered why they would leave me there all alone. I remember, it was very hot that day and I was getting very thirsty. As time passed, clouds started to hide the sun. It helped my thirst a little.

As nightfall came, I got scared, because it started to thunder and lightning. I couldn't go hide, or get under cover, because I was tied up. I had no place to go.

The rain was cold and wet....and the sky made a lot of Really Loud Noise!

The lightning was so bright that I could see all the trees bending.........

They seemed angry......

As I laid there getting wet and very cold, I wondered what was going to happen.

Would anyone come back for me?

But, someone did come. I could see them running towards me. I was huddled up, wet and shivering.

They untied me, picked me up, and wrapped me in a warm blanket.

They told me that I would be given to a new family. One that would love me and keep me safe.

That was when I came to live where I am now.
When I met my new parents, I saw that they were
much older than my last ones, but they were both
so nice to me.
I was given food, water and a new bed. They told
me I would never be punished for what someone
else did. They kept their promise. They were very
nice to me.

But, I want to talk about my Dad......not me right now. He was really big, but most of the time he was in a wheel chair, so he didn't look that big. I liked him right away. I could tell, he felt the same about me.

I would follow him around the house... When he would go in the bedroom to rest, I would be allowed to rest with him...
This was my very special time with him...
He would pet me and rub my ears and scratch my belly for a long time, usually until we would both fall asleep!

When he was in his wheel chair, during meal time, I would sit under his chair. Sometimes he would reach down and give me a taste too.
I would even sit outside the shower and wait for him... Sometimes I got wet!

No matter where he went in the house, I was right there too!
We watched television together, and I would sit with him while he played video games.
I was happy no matter where we were or what we did. We were inseparable!
When he had a snack, I had one too!

We had something very special together..
He helped me mend my fears.......I helped him accept his.

He had a big chair that laid back, a recliner, where he would also sit...
When he would recline in it, I would sit under the leg rest..
This is where he was when it happened.
That night everything changed forever...

It was late. We had been sleeping for awhile..
Dad had been restless all night.   Mom was worried, I could tell.
I heard her ask him if he was alright, and he said he was fine.

Later that night, Mom asked him again if he was o.k., but this time he didn't answer.
Mom got very upset... She was making phone calls, talking to Dad,
trying to wake him up... But, he wouldn't wake up.....

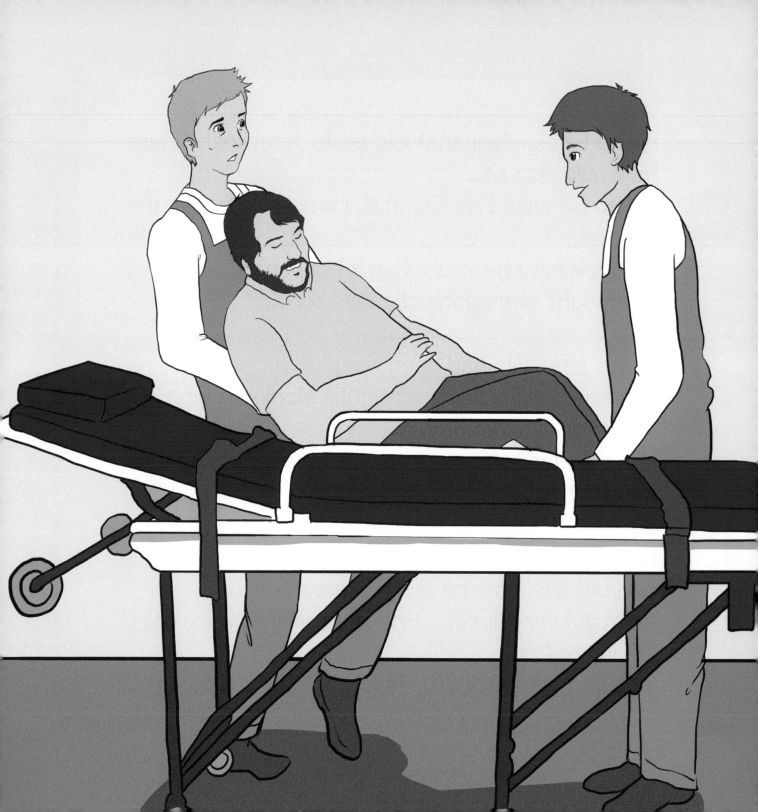

Soon there were people I didn't know in the house trying to wake Daddy too, but he still would not wake up.
They put him on a stretcher and carried him out, and Mom left too....

I didn't know what to do, so I just waited...
I got up in his recliner, and waited some more......
It was a long time before Mom came home...
She was sad.....I could tell.
It made me sad too.

The next few days I would get in his recliner and wait for him to return...
It made me feel close to him, even though he wasn't there..

As the days went by, Mom would cry and talk to me about Dad...
It was then I knew he was not coming home.......

It has been six months now...I still miss him a lot..I guess I always will...

But for awhile I had the best Dad in the world, and I have that to hold on to, along with all the memories we shared together.

He loved me, and I loved him, and I guess,------------ no,---------- I KNOW,   I always will!

Printed in the United States
By Bookmasters